CONTINENTS

Europe

Leila Merrell Foster

www.heinemann.co.uk/library

Visit our website to find out more information about Heinemann Library books.

To order:
☎ Phone 44 (0) 1865 888066
  Send a fax to 44 (0) 1865 314091
  Visit the Heinemann Bookshop at www.heinemann.co.uk/library to browse our
  catalogue and order online.

First published in Great Britain by Heinemann Library, Halley Court, Jordan Hill, Oxford OX2 8EJ, part of Harcourt Education. Heinemann is a registered trademark of Harcourt Education Ltd.

Editorial: Kathy Peltan, Clare Lewis, and Katie Shepherd
Design: Joanna Hinton-Malivoire and Q2A Creative
Picture research: Erica Newbery
Production: Helen McCreath

Origination: Modern Age Repro House Ltd.
Printed and bound in China by South China Printing Co. Ltd.

13-digit ISBN 978-0-431-15809-9 (hardback)
10 09 08 07 06
10 9 8 7 6 5 4 3 2 1

13-digit ISBN 978-0-431-09895-1 (paperback)
11 10 09 08 07
10 9 8 7 6 5 4 3 2 1

British Library Cataloguing in Publication Data

Foster, Leila Merrell
Europe. – 2nd ed. – (Continents)
914
A full catalogue record for this book is available from the British Library.

Acknowledgements

The publishers would like to thank the following for permission to reproduce photographs: Getty Images/Lonely Planet Images/ Graeme Cornwalls, p. **5**; Earth Scenes/P. O'Toole, p. **7**; Photo Edit/Tony Freeman, p. **9**; Tony Stone/Shaun Egan, p. **11**; Bruce Coleman, Inc./Olivier Lequeinec, p. **13**; Animals Animals/Darek Karp, p. **14**; Bruce Coleman, Inc./Wedlgo Ferchland, p. **15**; Corbis/Tony Arruza, p. **16**; Tony Stone/Michael Busselle, p. **17**; Getty/Lonely Planet Images/Jean-Bernard Carillet, p. **19**; Tony Stone/John Lamb, p. **21**; Bruce Coleman, Inc./Guido Cozzi, pp. **22**; Bruce Coleman, Inc./Masha Nordbye, p. **23**; Bruce Coleman, Inc./C. & J. McClurg, p. **24**; Corbis p. **25**; Bruce Coleman, Inc., p. **27**; Photo Edit/Bill Buchmann, p. **28**; Tony Stone/Arnold Husmo, p. **29**.

Cover photograph of Europe, reproduced with permission of Science Photo Library/ Tom Van Sant, Geosphere Project/ Planetary Visions.

The publishers would like to thank Kathy Peltan, Keith Lye, and Nancy Harris for their assistance in the preparation of this book.

Every effort has been made to contact copyright holders of any material reproduced in this book. Any omissions will be rectified in subsequent printings if notice is given to the publishers.

Some words are shown in bold, **like this**. You can find out what they mean by looking in the glossary.

Contents

Where is Europe?

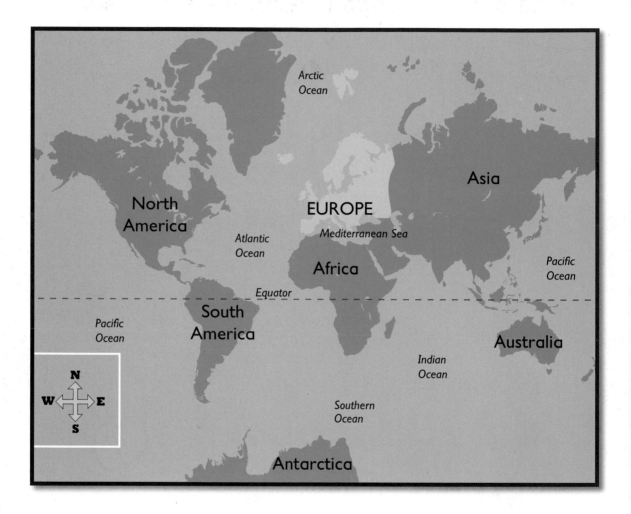

A continent is a very large area of land. There are seven continents. Europe is one of the smallest. To the north is the Arctic Ocean. The Atlantic Ocean is to the west. The Mediterranean Sea separates southern Europe from Africa.

To the east of Europe is Asia. Asia is a very large continent. The continent of Europe includes many **islands**. Most of these are very small and belong to larger countries. Some, such as Iceland, are **independent** countries. This means they do not belong to another country.

▲ *The island of Iceland is an independent European country*

Weather

Europe has many **climates**. A climate is the type of weather a place has. Land north of the **Arctic Circle** is always covered in ice. Countries in the south of Europe have warmer weather. It is warm and wet in winter. It is hot and dry in summer.

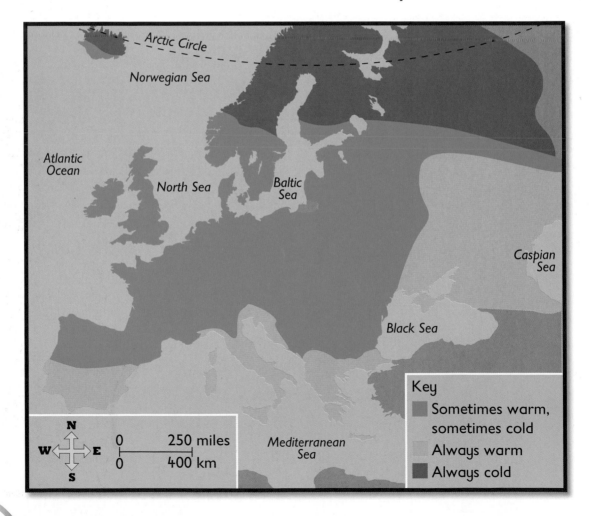

Arctic Circle

Norwegian Sea

Atlantic Ocean

North Sea

Baltic Sea

Caspian Sea

Black Sea

Mediterranean Sea

N
W   E
S

| 0 | 250 miles |
| 0 | 400 km |

Key
Sometimes warm, sometimes cold
Always warm
Always cold

Much of Europe does not get very cold in winter or very hot in summer. In western Europe, there are **currents** of warm water in the Atlantic Ocean. They stop **coastal** areas from becoming icy. Sometimes these places are rainy and misty.

▲ *Misty weather in Scotland*

Mountains

Europe has many high mountain **ranges**. The Ural Mountains are in the east. The Caucasus Mountains are in the south. They separate Europe from Asia. Mount Elbrus is the highest peak in Europe. It is in the Caucasus Mountains.

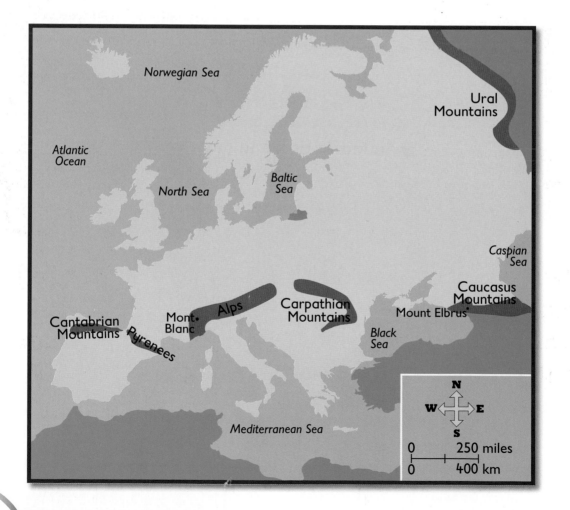

The Alps go through five different countries in Europe.

▲ *Jungfrau peak, in the Swiss Alps*

The Alps stretch for over 1,000 kilometres (620 miles) across southern Europe. The highest mountain in the Alps is Mont Blanc. There is a long tunnel underneath it. The tunnel helps cars to cross the Alps more easily.

Rivers

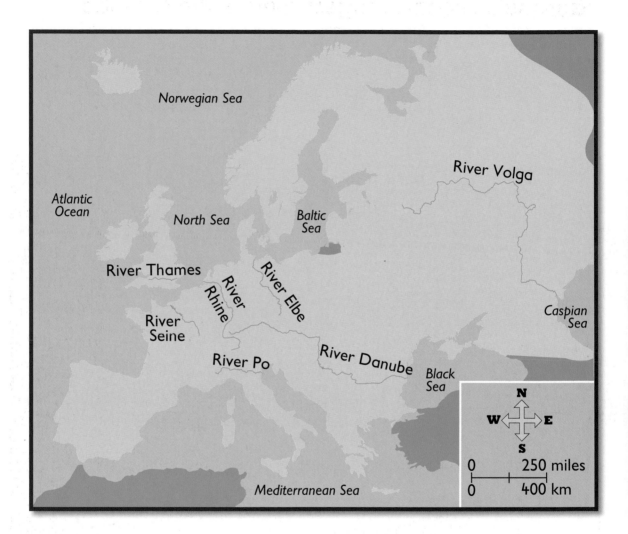

The longest river in Europe is the Volga, in Russia. It is usually frozen for three months each year. Ships can travel right across Europe because a **canal** links the River Rhine to the River Danube.

Europe's second longest river is the Danube. It flows through nine European countries. The **capital** cities of Vienna, Bratislava, Budapest, and Belgrade are all on the River Danube.

▲ *River Danube, in Budapest, Hungary*

Lakes

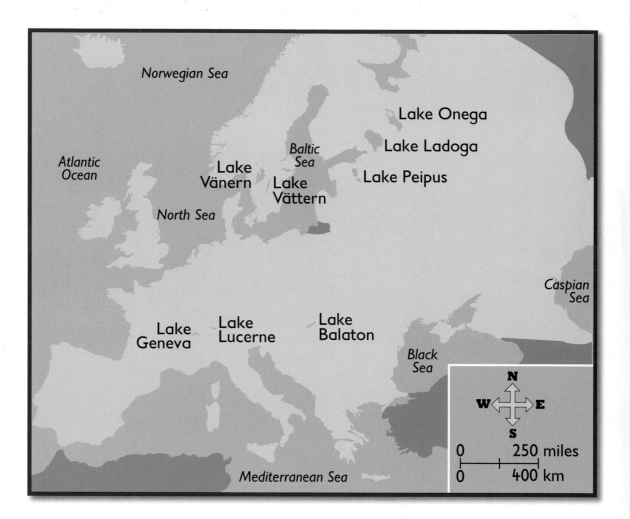

Europe has many large **freshwater** lakes. The largest is Lake Ladoga in Russia. In many lakes and rivers in Europe, the water is **polluted**. Waste from factories and farms is killing the fish that live in this water.

Switzerland has many beautiful lakes, such as Lake Geneva and Lake Lucerne. People often use these lakes for sailing and windsurfing. Water from some lakes is **treated** to make it safe to drink. Then the water is sent to people's homes.

▲ *Lake Geneva, Switzerland*

Animals

People used to hunt wild wolves and bears in Europe. Now there are only a few left. But many deer and foxes still live in the wild in Europe.

▲ *Grey wolf in Poland*

▲ *Reindeer herd in Sweden*

In the far north of Europe, people keep **herds** of reindeer for their meat, milk, and fur. Polar bears, whales, and seals also live in icy places. In the warm south, there are lizards and snakes.

Plants

Many farmers in Italy, Greece, and Spain grow olive trees. The olives are eaten whole, or **pressed** to make cooking oil. Orange and lemon trees also grow there. In the cooler Netherlands, some people grow fields of colourful flowers called tulips.

▲ *Olive trees in Spain*

▲ *Vineyard in France*

Grapes grow in fields called vineyards. Most vineyards are in sunny southern Europe. The grapes are crushed to make wine. In northern Europe there are forests of evergreen trees, such as pines.

Countries

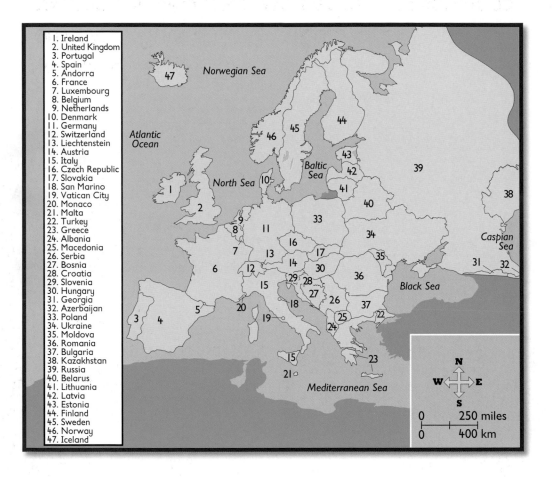

1. Ireland
2. United Kingdom
3. Portugal
4. Spain
5. Andorra
6. France
7. Luxembourg
8. Belgium
9. Netherlands
10. Denmark
11. Germany
12. Switzerland
13. Liechtenstein
14. Austria
15. Italy
16. Czech Republic
17. Slovakia
18. San Marino
19. Vatican City
20. Monaco
21. Malta
22. Turkey
23. Greece
24. Albania
25. Macedonia
26. Serbia
27. Bosnia
28. Croatia
29. Slovenia
30. Hungary
31. Georgia
32. Azerbaijan
33. Poland
34. Ukraine
35. Moldova
36. Romania
37. Bulgaria
38. Kazakhstan
39. Russia
40. Belarus
41. Lithuania
42. Latvia
43. Estonia
44. Finland
45. Sweden
46. Norway
47. Iceland

There are 42 countries that are completely in Europe. There are also five countries that are partly in Europe and partly in another continent. For example, part of Russia is in Europe and part of it is in Asia.

Most countries in Europe have their own language. Some countries have more than one language. The Russian and Greek languages have different letters from the ones used in English.

About 50 different languages are spoken in Europe.

Cities

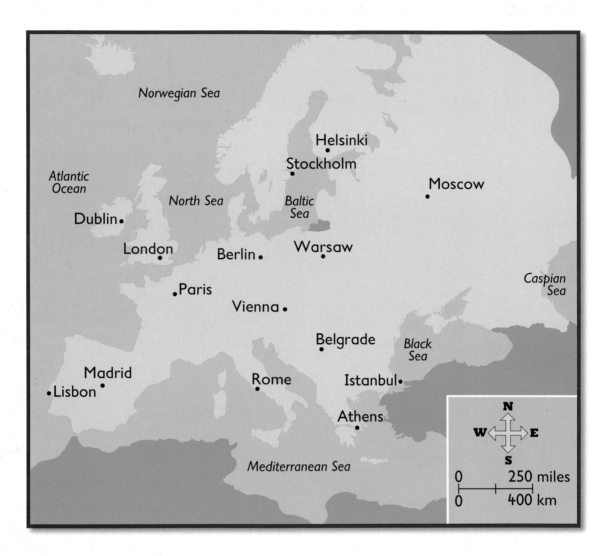

This map shows some of the most important cities in Europe. Paris is the **capital** of France. It is one of the world's most beautiful cities. It has beautiful buildings and wide, tree-lined streets called boulevards.

The capital of England is London. The Houses of Parliament are on the banks of the River Thames in London. The British **parliament** has met in the Houses of Parliament for over 700 years. Buckingham Palace is also in London. The Queen of England lives in the palace.

▼ *Houses of Parliament, London*

The Parthenon was built around 2,500 years ago.

▲ *The Parthenon, in Athens, Greece*

This ruined **temple** is called the Parthenon. The ancient Greeks built the temple for the Greek **goddess** Athena in the year 435 BC. People still follow the ideas of the great thinkers of ancient Athens.

Moscow is the **capital** of Russia. The leaders of Russia work in buildings called the Kremlin. The Kremlin is in Moscow's Red Square. The cathedral was built by Ivan the Terrible.

Kremlin

St Basil's cathedral

▲ Red Square, Moscow

In the country

All round the coast of Europe, people go fishing. In the cold northern seas, they catch cod, herring and haddock. In the warmer southern seas, they catch sardines, tuna, and shellfish.

▲ *Fishing boats in Portugal*

▲ *A large field of wheat*

Many farmers in Europe grow wheat. The wheat is ground into flour to make bread. In southern Europe, flour is also used to make pasta. Northern Europe also has many **dairy farms**. The milk from the cows is turned into butter and cheese.

Famous places

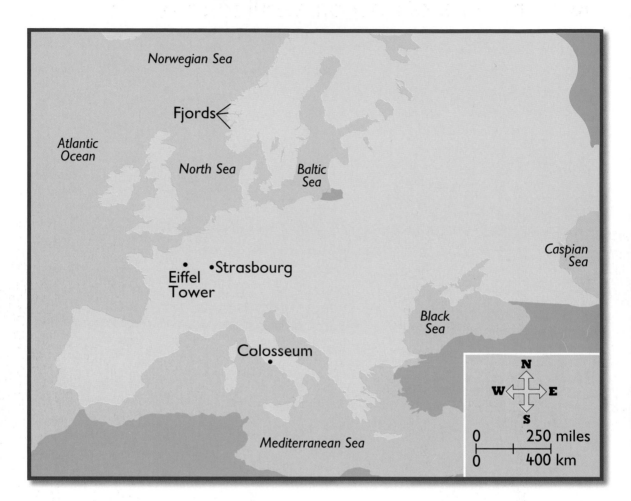

Many European countries have joined a group called the European Union, or EU. The 25 members discuss how the countries of Europe can work together. The European **Parliament** meets in Strasbourg, in France.

Roman emperors put on exciting shows in the Colosseum. Huge crowds came to watch warriors, called gladiators. The gladiators would fight animals and each other.

The Colosseum was built by the Ancient Romans almost 2,000 years ago.

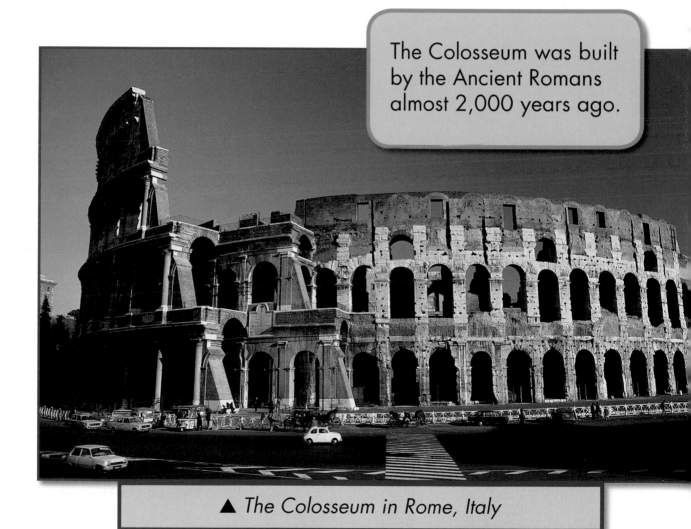

▲ *The Colosseum in Rome, Italy*

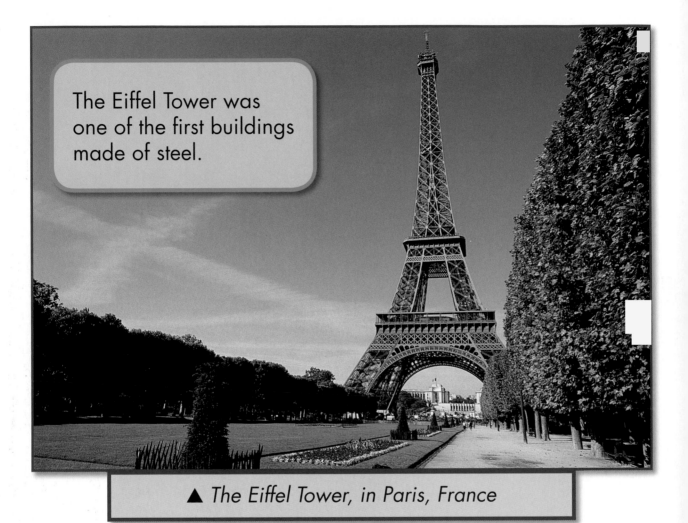

The Eiffel Tower was one of the first buildings made of steel.

▲ *The Eiffel Tower, in Paris, France*

For over 40 years, the Eiffel Tower was the tallest building in the world. Then, in 1931, the Empire State Building was built in New York City. Visitors take the lift or climb hundreds of stairs to reach the top of the Eiffel Tower.

The coast of Norway has hundreds of rocky fjords.

▲ *Troll fjord, Norway*

Fjords are deep channels that were cut into the rock by ice thousands of years ago. Large ships can use them to sail far inland.

Fast facts

Europe's longest rivers

Name of River	Length in kilometres	Length in miles	Begins	Flows through
Volga	3,700	2,300	Russia near Moscow	Russia
Danube	2,850	1,771	Germany	Central Europe
Dneiper	2,285	1,420	SW Russia	Belarus, Ukraine
Don	1,969	1,223	Russia near Moscow	Russia

Europe's highest mountains

Name and range	Height in metres	Height in feet	Country
Elbrus, Caucasus	5,633	18,481	Russia (Europe)
Mont Blanc, Alps	4,807	15,771	France, Italy
Pico de Aneto, Pyrenees	3,404	11,168	France, Spain
Gerlachovsky Peak, Carpathian	2,655	8,711	Slovakia

European record breakers

Europe is the most crowded continent in the world.

Europe has part of the largest country in the world, Russia.

Europe also has the world's smallest country, Vatican City. It is only less than half a square kilometre (under a quarter of a square mile).

The Saint Gotthard tunnel in central Switzerland is the world's longest tunnel for motor traffic. It is 16.3 kilometres (10.1 miles) long.

Finland has 60,000 lakes. It is known as the "land of thousands of lakes".

Glossary

Arctic Circle imaginary line that circles the earth near the North Pole

canal man-made waterway

capital city where government leaders work

climate type of weather a place has

coastal near the coast

current strong movement of water

dairy farm farm where cows or goats are kept for their milk

freshwater water that is not salty

goddess female god. The ancient Greeks had many gods and goddesses.

herd large group of animals, such as reindeer

independent country that is free to make its own laws

island land that is surrounded by water

parliament group of people who make the laws of their country

polluted poisoned or damaged by something harmful

pressed squeezed to make juice or oil come out

range line of mountains that are connected to each other

temple place built to worship a god or goddess. People often go there to pray.

treated when chemicals have been used to make something clean and free from germs

More books to read

My World of Geography: Rivers, Angela Royston
(Heinemann Library, 2004)

Watching Reindeer in Europe, Elizabeth Miles (Heinemann Library, 2006)

We're from Italy, Emma Lynch (Heinemann Library, 2005)

Index